MW01126756

A COMMENTARY ON EPHESIANS

By

Charles H. Spurgeon

Charles H. Spurgeon's Ephesians Commentary Contents

FOREWORD

Charles Haddon Spurgeon (1834-92) is known as the Prince of Preachers because of his extraordinary gift as a preacher of God's word. His ability was God-given and he used it for the glory of his Lord.

He gave his heart and life to Christ at the age of 15 after being forced to seek shelter from a snow storm in a Methodist chapel. Spurgeon was only 19 when he was called into full-time ministry as pastor of New Park Street Chapel. This Church, of course, eventually grew through God's grace which necessitated it moving to newly built premises and took the new name of the Metropolitan Tabernacle.

Spurgeon is most often remembered as being a preacher with little emphasis placed on other areas of his ministry. He was responsible for facilitating the opening of an orphanage, a college for training pastors and greatly supported the selling of Christian books. His ministry was anything but one-sided!

What we should remember is that Spurgeon communicated God's word and he was happy to use any medium that was available to him. His written works were invaluable as they were available to the many people who were unable to hear him preach. Indeed his volume, "Lectures To My Students" was published and as well as general sale copies were provided to many ministers around the country at their request and at the expense of Susannah Spurgeon who administered a fund to facilitate this generosity.

This book you are holding is not the product of Spurgeon's writing ministry nor the result of his preaching. These words are all Spurgeon's and they came about as the result of him expounding a chapter of the Bible during his Sunday service. Such was his gift that he could do this with very little specific preparation. He would select a chapter and tell the congregation the salient points and matters contained therein.

It is not a complete commentary of Scripture, indeed many chapters of the Bible did not receive this attention from him. Indeed in this commentary on Ephesians he had not provided an exegesis on chapter 4. But what Spurgeon left was a legacy of inspired, accurate and valuable insights into Scripture. These words you will read are for the preacher but, and more importantly, they are for every Christian. We pray that you will find that they help open Scripture to you in a new way.

We make use of commentaries, lexicons and concordances to help us better understand God's word. But these tools must never supplant or replace the Bible. There is no substitute to reading His word in order that we might apply it to our own lives.

Every blessing in the name of our Lord, Jesus Christ.

EPHESIANS CHAPTER 1

Verse 1
Ephesians 1:1-2. Paul, an apostle of Jesus Christ by the will of God, to the saints which are at Ephesus, and to the faithful in Christ Jesus: Grace be to you, and peace, from God our Father, and from the Lord Jesus Christ.
He wishes them grace, first, and peace afterwards, which is the right and natural order. There is no lasting peace without grace. There is no peace worth having which does not spring from a work of grace in the soul. "Grace be to you, and peace from God our Father, and from the Lord Jesus Christ."

Ephesians 1:3. Blessed be the God and Father of our Lord Jesus Christ,
How dear the Father is when we view him in association with the Redeemer. Never do the saints seem to delight so much in God as when they behold him in the person of Jesus Christ. Then is he inexpressibly lovely to us, and we preach him with joy and delight. "Blessed be the God and Father of our Lord Jesus Christ."

Ephesians 1:3. Who have blessed us with all spiritual blessings in heavenly places in Christ:
"Blessed," says he, "be God, who hath blessed us." Well may we bless him with our feeble thanks who has blest us with his might; mercies. Nothing makes a man bless God like God's blessing him. "He has blessed us," says the apostle, "with all spiritual blessings." The children of God have not only some blessings, but all they want. They are all theirs — all for time and all for eternity, but they are all in Christ. There is no blessing out of Christ. All the fullness of blessing dwells in Jesus, and in him only. And if thou wouldest be blessed, thou must come to Christ for a blessing. He has "blest us with all spiritual blessings in heavenly places in Christ."

Ephesians 1:4. According as he hath chosen us in him before the foundation of the world, that we should be holy and without blame before him in love:
The first great blessing of the covenant of grace is our election. We were chosen, but chosen in Christ — chosen not because we were holy, but chosen that we should be holy. The great object of the divine choice is our holiness. And let no man say that he is chosen of God unless God is working in him to this divine end, namely, holiness of character.

Ephesians 1:5. Having predestinated us unto the adoption of children by Jesus Christ to himself, according to the good pleasure of his will,
After election comes adoption. Men are not by nature the children of God but they are heirs of wrath. And this is very clear, because a man never adopts his own children. But adoption in itself proves that by nature we are not the children of God, but he adopts us. "Then are ye begotten again unto a lively hope by the resurrection of Jesus Christ from the dead." Happy they who know their adoption — who feel in themselves the spirit of children, and can cry, "Abba, Father," as they look up to God tonight. This is in Christ Jesus, for nothing comes to us except by him.

Ephesians 1:6. To the praise of the glory of his grace, wherein he hath made us accepted in the beloved.
Christ is so acceptable to God that that acceptance is sufficient to spread over all those who are in him. And tonight every believer here is accepted before God, but it is through Jesus Christ. Do notice that. Nothing comes but by that silver pipe. "He hath made us accepted in the Beloved."

Ephesians 1:7. In whom we have redemption through his blood, the forgiveness of sins, according to the riches of his grace;
Redemption by Christ, forgiveness by Christ, still everything through the Crucified. Those dear wounds of his are the five sacred founts from which a world of blessing flows to bless poor needy sinners. Well may we say, "None but Christ," for, indeed, there is none but Christ who can bless us.

Ephesians 1:8-10. Wherein he hath abounded toward us in all wisdom and prudence; Having made known unto us the mystery of his will, according to his good pleasure which he hath purposed in himself, that in the dispensation of the fullness of times he might gather together in one all things in Christ, both which are in heaven, and which are on earth: even in him:
All the things that are in Christ are to be gathered together — believing Jews no longer to be divided from believing Gentiles. Today the Church of God is separated — disfigured and weakened by divers sects and parties, but it shall not be always so. There is a gathering under the Christ, and he will in the fullness of time perfectly accomplish it.

Ephesians 1:11-12. In whom also we have obtained an inheritance, being predestinated according to the purpose of him who worketh all things after the counsel of his own will: That we should be to the praise of his glory, who first trusted in Christ.
Some people are dreadfully frightened at that word "predestination." I am always astonished when members of the Church of England are so, for if they will turn to their own articles, they will find that the high end comfortable doctrine of predestination is there taught. It is to be wisely handled, but it is not to be gagged and sent into a corner, as it is by some. Are there truths in Scripture that are not to be taught? If any say so then I charge him with being like the Jesuit, who hides a part of what he believes. Nay, the whole of God's truth is to be declared, and whatsoever we find in this book, that are we to state, and the keeping back of precious truth will be required of such as are guilty of it at the last great day.

Ephesians 1:13 to Ephesians 2:1. In whom ye also trusted, after that ye heard the word of truth, the gospel of your salvation in whom also, after that ye believed, ye were sealed with that Holy Spirit of promise, Which is the earnest of our inheritance until the redemption of the purchased possession, unto the praise of his glory. Wherefore I also, after I heard of your faith in the

Lord Jesus, and love unto all the saints, Cease not to give thanks for you, making mention of you in my prayers; That the God of our Lord Jesus Christ, the Father of glory, may give unto you the spirit of wisdom and revelation in the knowledge of him: The eyes of your understanding being enlightened; that ye may know what is the hope of his calling, and what the riches of the glory of his inheritance in the saints, And what is the exceeding greatness of his power to us-ward who believe, according to the working of his mighty power. Which he wrought in Christ, when be raised him from the dead, and set him at his own right hand in the heavenly places, Far above all principality, and power, and might, and dominion, and every name that is named, not only in this world, but also in that which is to come: And hath put all things under his feet, and gave him to be the head over all things to the church, Which is his body, the fullness of him that filleth all in all. And you hath he quickened, who were dead in trespasses and sins;

So that what he did for Christ he has done for you. He raised him and he has raised you, and, having begun thus to quicken you, he will go on to lift you up and to exalt you till you sit with him upon his throne. The only question, dear friends, is this. Do we belong to these of whom Paul here speaks? We look to the first verse to see who they are, and we find he is addressing the faithful in Christ Jesus; that is, those who are believing in Christ Jesus. If we are believing in him, then all the privileges, which are mentioned in this Chapter belong to us, and we are quickened and we shall be exalted even as Christ is, at the Father's right hand. So be it, gracious Lord.

Verses 1-14

In this chapter, we see what Paul, writing under the inspiration of the Holy Spirit, has to say about the possessions and privileges of believers in the Lord Jesus Christ.

Ephesians 1:1-2. Paul, an apostle of Jesus Christ by the will of God, to the saints which are at Ephesus, and to the faithful in Christ Jesus: Grace be to you, and peace, from God our Father, and from the Lord Jesus Christ. Brethren and sisters in Christ, this is a benediction for you as well as for the saints at Ephesus; it is for all "the faithful in Christ Jesus." May you all have grace without measure, and may you all have "the peace of God, which passeth all understanding," to "keep your hearts and minds through Christ Jesus"! Grace and peace are both to be had by believing in Jesus.

Ephesians 1:3. Blessed be the God and Father of our Lord Jesus Christ, who hath blessed us with all spiritual blessings in heavenly places in Christ:
It is right that we should bless God as he has so richly blessed us. Blessed be the Heavenly Father who has so abundantly blessed his children. How has he blessed us? "With all spiritual blessings in heavenly places (or, things) in Christ."

Ephesians 1:4. According as he hath chosen us in him before the foundation of the world,
That is the commencement of all the blessing, God's electing love. This is the fountain from which the living waters flow. There would have been no stream of blessing to us at all if it had not been for this first primeval choice of us by God, even as Jesus said to his disciples, "Ye have not chosen me, but I have chosen you."

Ephesians 1:4. That we should be holy and without blame before him in love:
Here is the blessing of sanctification; we are chosen that we may be made holy. To what nobler end could we have been elected? Is not this the very highest of our heart's desires, — "that we should be holy and without blame before him in love"?

Ephesians 1:5. Having predestinated us unto the adoption of children by Jesus Christ to himself, according to the good pleasure of his will,
Oh, what a blessing this is, altogether inconceivable in its results!
"Behold what wondrous grace,
The Father hath bestow'd
On sinners of a mortal race,
To call them sons of God!"

Ephesians 1:6. To the praise of the glory of his grace, wherein he hath made us accepted in the beloved.
There is music for you: "accepted in the Beloved." Are there grander words in any language than those four? Oh, the joy of being beloved, adopted, accepted by God the Father because of his beloved Son! Now comes something more: —

Ephesians 1:7. In whom we have redemption through his blood, the forgiveness of sins, according to the riches of his grace;
Redemption from destruction, the forgiveness of our sins, — we have all this through "the riches of his grace."

Ephesians 1:8-14. Wherein he hath abounded toward us in all wisdom and prudence; having made known unto us the mystery of his will, according to his good pleasure which he hath purposed in himself: that in the dispensation of the fullness of times he might gather together in one all things in Christ, both which are in heaven, and which are on earth; even in him: in whom also we have obtained an inheritance, being predestinated according to the purpose of him who worketh all things after the counsel of his own will: that we should be to the praise of his glory, who first trusted in Christ. In whom ye also trusted, after that ye heard the word of truth, the gospel of your salvation: in whom also after that ye believed, ye were sealed with that holy Spirit of promise, which is the earnest of our inheritance until the redemption of the purchased possession, unto the praise of his glory.

There is no end to the blessing which God gives to his chosen. He is always blessing us with blessings upon blessings, grace upon grace, and then there will be glory to crown it all. Blessed be his holy name forever and ever.

Verses 1-23

Ephesians 1:1. Paul, an apostle of Jesus Christ by the will of God,
He was not made an apostle by man, neither did he take the office upon himself, but he was made an apostle by the will of God.

Ephesians 1:1. To the saints which are at Ephesus, and to the faithful in Christ Jesus:
The saints in Ephesus, the saints where they cried, "Great is Diana of the Ephesians," had to bear an earnest witness against idolatry. And, dear friends, today saints in London will not have a very easy time of it if they are faithful to their Lord, for there is much to protest against in this evil generation; but as there were holy ones in Ephesus, God grant that there may be many such in London.

Ephesians 1:2. Grace be to you, and peace, from God our Father, and from the Lord Jesus Christ.
Paul would have us peaceful, restful, quiet. That peace must be based upon grace, He does not pray that we may have peace apart from grace, but "Grace be to you, and peace."

Ephesians 1:3-4. Blessed be the God and Father of our Lord Jesus Christ, who hath blessed us with all spiritual blessings in heavenly places in Christ: According as he hath chosen us in him before the foundation of the world,
The high mystery of election is taught in the Word of God, but some are afraid to speak of it. Not so our Apostle. He brings it out very clearly and distinctly, and so should we, only taking care to keep it in the proportion of other doctrines.

Ephesians 1:4-5. That we should be holy and without blame before him in love. Having predestinated us unto the adoption of children by Jesus Christ to himself, according to the good pleasure of his will.
You hear much about the free will of man, hear a little about the free will of God. You would think, from the talk of some, that God was man's debtor and must needs do according to the will of man. But it is not so. He is a sovereign, and gives his grace where he chooses, and he would have us know that it is according to the good pleasure of his will.

Ephesians 1:6. To the praise of the glory of his grace, wherein he hath made us accepted in the beloved.
Are there four words in any language which contain choicer meaning than these, "Accepted in the Beloved"? Oh! if you can say that, if you can feel it to be true, you are among the happiest of men and women. "Accepted in the

Beloved." You can never be accepted apart from Christ, the Father's best Beloved. But there is merit enough in him to overflow and cover all our sins, and we are accepted in the Beloved.

Ephesians 1:7. In whom we have redemption through his blood, the forgiveness of sins, according to the riches of his grace:
Notice how the Apostle keeps on insisting that we have everything in Christ. He says, times out of number, "in him," "in Christ." We have redemption. We are free. We are under bonds no longer. What is the price? "Through his blood." What is the result? "Forgiveness of sins." What is the measure of our liberty? "According to the riches of his grace."

Ephesians 1:8. Wherein he hath abounded toward us in all wisdom and prudence;
Not drowning us with floods of his grace, but handing it out to us as we are able to take it. The riches of his grace we have, but he uses wisdom and prudence, teaching us little by little as we are able to bear it, and raising us up by degrees from one stage of grace to another, according as our poor frames can endure the joy.

Ephesians 1:9-10. Having made known unto us the mystery of his will, according to his good pleasure which he hath purposed in himself: That in the dispensation of the fullness of times he might gather together in one all things in Christ, both which are in heaven, and which are on earth; even in him:
There are things in Christ in heaven: there the things in Christ on earth; but all the things in Christ shall be gathered together. All the redeemed shall come as one great host to bow before the throne of the infinite Majesty.

Ephesians 1:11. In whom also
Notice those words.

Ephesians 1:11. We have obtained an inheritance,
We have got the inheritance. Even now we have entered upon possession of the kingdom of grace.

Ephesians 1:11-12. Being predestinated according to the purpose of him who worketh all things after the counsel of his own will; That we should be to the praise of his glory, who first trusted in Christ.
The first saints led the way in the front of the army, and they are to the praise of God's glory to this day. We thank God for the apostles and martyrs who went before us. We will follow them as they followed Christ.

Ephesians 1:13. In whom ye also trusted, after that ye heard the word of truth, the gospel of your salvation: in whom also after that ye believed, ye were sealed with that holy Spirit of promise.

After faith, the Holy Spirit is given to dwell in the soul. That is the seal. It is not that the Holy Spirit brings a seal with him. He is the seal. Where he dwells, he is the seal of God's love to that man.

Ephesians 1:14. Which is the earnest of our inheritance until the redemption of the purchased possession, unto the praise of his glory.
The Holy Ghost is first the seal, and next the earnest. We all know what an earnest is. It is different from a pledge. A pledge is given, and then it is taken back again when the stipulation is carried out, but an earnest is part of what is to be received ultimately. The man who receives an earnest of his wage gets a few shillings, say, on Thursday, instead of taking all on Saturday. He never returns that. It is a part of his wage. And so the Holy Ghost is a part of him. When we have got him, we have got Christ.
"Thou art the earnest of his love,
The pledge of joys to come;
And thy soft wings, Celestial Dove,
Shall safe convey me home."

Ephesians 1:15-16. Wherefore I also, after I heard of your faith in the Lord Jesus, and love unto all the saints, Cease not to give thanks for you, making mention of you in my prayers;
Is that the way that we pray? Do we make mention of people in our prayers? It is well to do so. It is a good plan to keep a list of persons for whom we ought to pray, and to put it before us when we draw near to God, and go over the names. I knew one man of God who has kept a debtor and creditor list with God for many years. He puts his requests down in the book, and when they are answered he writes that down. If they are not answered he repeats them. It is a very wonderful book. I think that he told me that there is a name down there of a person for whom he has prayed, and that he is not converted yet. Out of several for whom he began to pray, he is the only one who is not converted, and is the only one that is left alive. The others were brought to Christ, and died in the faith, and he, not yet brought to Christ, still lives. He prays on with as great a confidence of the conversion of that man as I have that Christmas will come in due time. I wish that we did business with God in some such fashion as that, but our prayers are shadowy, unreal. God teach us how to pray!

Ephesians 1:17-18. That the God of our Lord Jesus Christ, the Father of glory, may give unto you the spirit of wisdom and revelation in the knowledge of him: The eyes of your understanding being enlightened; that ye may know what is the hope of his calling,
You see he gave thanks to God for their faith and for their love. But there are three divine sisters that must never be separated — faith, hope, and love, and so the Apostle prays, "that ye may know what is the hope of his calling."

Ephesians 1:18-21. And what the riches of the glory of his inheritance in the saints. And what is the exceeding greatness of his power to us-ward who believe, according to he working of his mighty power, Which he wrought in Christ, when he raised him from the dead, and set him at his own right hand in the heavenly places, Far above all principality, and power, and might, and dominion, and every name that is named, not only in this world, but also in that which is to come:
See how high Christ is raised! The same power that brought Christ from the dead, and set him on high, works in the salvation of every believer. Nothing less than omnipotence can save a soul; and omnipotence at its very best in the glorification of Christ is none too great for the salvation of a sinner.

Ephesians 1:22-23. And hath put all things under his feet, and gave him to be the head over all things to the church, Which is his body, the fullness of him that filleth all in all.
May God bless to us the reading of that chapter.
This exposition consisted of readings from 1 Corinthians 13; Ephesians 1.

EPHESIANS CHAPTER 2

Verses 1-22

Ephesians 2:1. And you hath he quickened, who were dead in trespasses and sins:

These were your grave clothes. You were wrapped up in them. Nay, this was your sarcophagus. You were shut up in it, as in a great stone coffin: "Dead in trespasses and sins."

Ephesians 2:2. Wherein in time past ye walked according to the course of this world, according to the prince of the power of the air, the spirit that now worketh in the children of disobedience.

You were once no better than the workshop of the devil. He is the spirit that worketh in the children of disobedience, as the smith works in his forge. When you hear foul language, when you see bad actions, these are the sparks coming out of the chimney that let you know who is at work within, down below. What a dreadful thing it is — a man dead to all that is good, but alive through the indwelling of the devil that is within him. "The spirit that now worketh in the children of disobedience."

Ephesians 2:3. Among whom also we all had our conversation in times past in the lusts of our flesh, fulfilling the desires of the flesh and of the mind; and were by nature the children of wrath, even as others.

Not children of God, even as some profanely assert when they talk about the universal fatherhood of God. Ye were children of wrath, even as others. And the best of men were no better than ethers by nature. They were as dead, as much under the influence of Satan, as much under the influence of the lusts of the flesh as others are who are left where they are. It is only sovereign grace that makes us to differ. "Were by nature," not by error; by nature, not by a mistake, not by a few actions, but by nature, the children of wrath, even as others. See what you used to be. Let this make you humble. See what you would have been. Let this make you grateful. "You hath he quickened." He has put life into you. He has made you quit your graves. He has made you come from under the dominion of Satan and the devices of your own heart. Will you not bless his name tonight?

Ephesians 2:4-5. But God, who is rich in mercy, for his great love wherewith he loved us, even when we were dead in sins, hath quickened us together with Christ,

Wonder! The life that quickens. Christ quickens all the members of his mystical body, and this has come to us through the riches of God's mercy. Whatever God has, he has in abundance, but of his mercy we read that he has riches of it; and truly all those riches of mercy he has shown in our case. We cannot but have riches of gratitude for such riches of mercy.

Ephesians 2:5. (By grace ye are saved;)

See, Paul puts that in a parenthesis. It was not necessary to the sense, but he knew that there would come a time when men would not like this doctrine, so he puts it in, "by grace are ye saved." They cannot bear it, and therefore they shall have it. They shall have it when the sense does not seem to demand it. To make it quite clear, he will insert it, "by grace ye are saved."

Ephesians 2:6. And hath raised us up together, and made us sit together in heavenly places in Christ Jesus.
We are not only raised from the dead with Christ, but we are spiritually raised into the heavenly places with him. It is a great thing when a man learns to look up from earth to heaven. It is a greater thing when he learns to look down from heaven upon earth — to have you sitting at the right hand of God, and then to look down on all the things of this present life as far below you.

Ephesians 2:7. That in the ages to come he might show the exceeding riches of his grace in his kindness toward us through Christ Jesus.
Brethren, we are to be a show, an exhibition case, in which God will exhibit the riches of his grace in his kindness toward us through Christ Jesus. Angels will count it a high joy to study the life of a regenerate man, to see him rise from death in sin to the glory of God in Christ Jesus. What is so precious in God's esteem ought to excite our praise continually.

Ephesians 2:8. For by grace are ye saved
There it is again. Paul rings that silver bell in the deaf ears of men. "By grace are ye saved."

Ephesians 2:8-9. Through faith; and that not of yourselves: it is the gift of God: Not of works, lest any man should boast.
We should be sure to boast if we could. We are a boasting people. Man is a poor mass of flesh, and he is largely given to the corruption of pride, He will boast if he can.

Ephesians 2:10. For we are his workmanship,
If there is any good thing in us, he put it there. It is not for us to boast. It is for him to boast if he pleases.

Ephesians 2:10-11. Created in Christ Jesus unto good works, which God hath before ordained that we should walk in them. Wherefore remember,
Oh! that is a good word for us, "Remember," we are so apt to forget. "Remember."

Ephesians 2:11-12. That ye being in time past Gentiles in the flesh, who are called Uncircumcision by that which is called the Circumcision in the flesh made by hands; that at that time ye were without Christ,
Had you to do with Christ? The Jews call you uncircumcised dogs. What had you to do with the Messiah? Was not the Messiah for God's Israel? You did not belong to Israel.

Ephesians 2:12. Being aliens from the commonwealth of Israel, and strangers from the covenants of promise,
The covenant was in Isaac. You are not the children of Isaac. You are not descended from Abraham. You were strangers from the covenants of promise.

Ephesians 2:12. Having no hope,
Either here or hereafter.

Ephesians 2:12-13. And without God in the world:
But now Oh! what a contrast.

Ephesians 2:13. In Christ Jesus ye who sometimes were far off are made nigh by the blood of Christ.
You are brought near to Israel. You are brought nearer still to Israel's God. Now you are not aliens. You are not strangers from the covenant. You have a hope, you have a God.

Ephesians 2:14-15. For he is our peace, who hath made both one, and hath broken down the middle wall of partition between us; having abolished in his flesh the enmity, even the law of commandments contained in ordinances; for to make in himself of twain one new man, so making peace;
There is no circumcision and uncircumcision now, for that is done away with. There is no Israel according to the flesh now, and Gentiles who are not of God, for there is a spiritual Israel, to which we belong, as well as those of Abraham's race. He has swept out of the way all the ordinances which divided us, and we are now one in him.

Ephesians 2:16-17. And that he might reconcile both unto God in one body by the cross, having slain the enmity thereby: and came and preached peace to you which were afar off, and to them that were nigh.
To the Gentile and to the Jew, to the atrociously wicked, and to those who were religious after a fashion — he has brought them both in by the cross.

Ephesians 2:18. For through him we both have access by one Spirit unto the Father.
Here you have the Trinity in a single line of Scripture, and it needs the Trinity to make an acceptable prayer. Through him (that is, Christ) we have access by one Spirit unto the Father, and now, today, the Church of God is one in prayer, whether Jew or Gentile. We come to God by the same Mediator, helped by the same Spirit. We have answers of peace from the same Father.

Ephesians 2:19. Now therefore ye are no more strangers and foreigners, but fellowcitizens with the saints and of the household of God:
There are many here whom we do not know. We have not seen their faces before, but if they are in Christ and we are in Christ, we are very near of kin.

There is an old proverb that blood is thicker than water, and depend upon it that when there is the blood of Christ sprinkled upon us, it makes very near kinship. When we are bought with the same price, quickened by the same life, and are on the way to the same heaven, we are very near of kin. We are no mere strangers and foreigners, but fellowcitizens with the saints and all the household of God. They make a great fuss when they give a man the liberty of the City of London. There is a fine gold box to put it in. You have got the liberty of the new Jerusalem, and your faith, like a golden box, holds the deeds of your freemanship. Take care of them, and rejoice in them.

Ephesians 2:20-21. And are built upon the foundation of the apostles and prophets, Jesus Christ himself being the chief corner stone: in whom all the building fitly framed together groweth unto an holy temple in the Lord:
The church is a framed house. It has an architect. Some seem to think that it is a load of bricks. They have no church officers. There are none set apart to this work, and none to the other. It seems to be just a heap of stones thrown down anyhow. But a true church is, by the Spirit of God, a building fitly framed together. One is a door, another is a window. One lies low and hidden in the foundation. Another may have a more prominent position in the wall; and it should be so with us — that we should each have a place that God has appointed him, and keep to that place. Lord, build up thy Church upon earth at this time.

Ephesians 2:22. In whom ye also are builded together for an habitation of God through the Spirit.
We are not builded to stand like a carcase. It is a ghastly sight to see houses in London nearly finished, but never occupied: but it is the glory of the Church of God that it is inhabited. It is a habitation of God through the Spirit. Holy Spirit, dwell in thy Church more evidently. Keep open house for all poor sinners that come to Christ, and glorify God.

EPHESIANS CHAPTER 4

Verses 1-32

Ephesians 4:1. I therefore, the prisoner of the Lord, beseech you that ye walk worthy of the vocation wherewith ye are called,-

"You are called to be sons of God, you are called to be one with Christ, you are called to be kings and priests unto God; this is the highest possible vocation that anyone can have, so walk worthy of it." O beloved, if we walk worthy of this vocation, what holy and noble lives we shall lead! The apostle so much desired godliness and holiness to be the characteristics of those to whom he wrote that he used a very strong term of entreaty: "I beseech you that ye walk worthy of the vocation wherewith ye are called,-

Ephesians 4:2. With all lowliness and meekness, with long suffering, forbearing one another in love;-"

You are not called to hector over men, to be lords over God's heritage; you are called to be Christ-like, to be gentle and tender, ready to bear and to forgive all manner of wrong that may be done to you;"

Ephesians 4:3. Endeavoring to keep the unity of the Spirit in the bond of peace.

Some people seem as if they endeavored to break the unity of the Spirit, and to snap every sacred bond of love and Christian affection; be ye not like unto them, but let Christ's mind be in you; and with lowliness, and meekness, and longsuffering, endeavor to keep the unity of the Spirit in the bond of peace.

Ephesians 4:4-6. There is one body, and one Spirit, even as ye are called in one hope of your calling; one Lord, one faith, one baptism, one God and Father of all, who is above all, and through all, and in you all.

If there were two lords, you might be divided into two parties; if there were two faiths, you might split up into two sections; if there were two baptisms, you might be right in having two denominations; if there were two fathers, there might be two families; if there were two indwelling spirits, there would be, and there must be, two sorts of people; but, in the true Church of Jesus Christ, there is "one God and Father of all, who is above all, and through all, and in you all."

Ephesians 4:7. But unto every one of us is given grace according to the measure of the gift of Christ.

We have not all the same form of grace, and we cannot all perform the same service for the Saviour; we differ very much from each other as to our abilities, and as to the positions which we can occupy; and our Lord intended it to be so.

Ephesians 4:8-10. Wherefore he saith, When he ascended up on high, he led captivity captive. and gave gifts unto men. (Now that he ascended, what is it but that he also descended first into the lower parts of the earth? He that

descended is the same also that ascended up far above all heavens, that he might fill all things.)
Paul could not help giving us this lesson by the way, that he that ascended was also he that first descended; and you may depend upon it that the man who will attain the highest honour in the Church of Christ is the man who descends, who lays aside all ambition, and all desire to be honoured and respected, and who is willing to be nothing. He who thus descends, shall surely ascend.

Ephesians 4:11. And he gave some, apostles; and some, prophets; and some, evangelists; and some, pastors and teachers;
Not all alike, not all apostles or prophets; and not all equals, for pastors may not be equal in rank with apostles. They are not all to do the same work, for all teachers cannot prophesy, neither does a prophet always pasteurize, and watch over a flock. Jesus Christ gave divers gifts,-

Ephesians 4:12-13. For the perfecting of the saints, for the work of the ministry, for the edifying of the body of Christ: till we all come in the unity of the faith, and of the knowledge of the Son of God, unto a perfect man, unto the measure of the stature of the fullness of Christ.
Then, whatever spiritual gifts we have, they are not our own to use as we please; they are only entrusted to us that we may employ them to help our fellow-Christians. Beloved brethren and sisters, we are one with Christ, and we are one with each other; and, therefore, we must not look every man upon his own things, but also upon the things of others; and it should be a question of the first importance to every Christian, "How can I best utilize myself for the benefit of the rest of the members of the Church?" Do not ask, "How can I benefit myself?" but let your enquiry be, "How can I be most profitable to my fellow-Christians?" I have heard some professors say of a sermon that they could not feed under it; the discourse was very likely to be useful to the unconverted, but they could not hear it because they could not feed under it. Their idea seems to be that preaching must always be a spoon used for feeding them; but it is not so. The Word of God contains much spiritual nutriment specially suitable for the lambs of the flock. These men, who are strong, want meat, so they say that they do not enjoy what they hear, it is of no use to them. But are the babes in Christ's family never to be fed? Does not humanity itself teach us that, first of all, the weakest and feeblest should be cared for? Oh, for grace to be unselfish! There is such a thing as Christian selfishness; and, of all evil things in the world, it is the most unchristian. When the first and last concern of a man is his own salvation, his own comfort, his own advancement, his own edification, and nothing besides, he needs to be saved from such a selfish spirit as that.

Ephesians 4:14-16. That we henceforth be no more children, tossed to and fro, and carried about with every wind of doctrine, by the sleight of men, and cunning craftiness, whereby they lie in wait to deceive; but speaking the truth in love, 'may grow up into him in all things, which is the head even Christ: from whom the 'whole body fitly joined together and compacted by that which every joint supplieth, according to the effectual working in the measure of every part, maketh increase of the body unto the edifying of itself in love.

Every part of the body has its own special function; there are some secret vessels of which as yet the physiologists know very little. What may be the particular use of them has not yet been ascertained; but depend upon it, God has created no part of our body in vain; and, in like manner, in the mystical body of Christ, every Christian man has his own office, his own work, something that he can do that nobody else can do; and our great object should be to find out what that work is, and to give our whole strength to it, for the nourishing of the entire body of Christ.

Ephesians 4:17-19. This I say therefore, and testify in the Lord, that ye henceforth walk not as other Gentiles walk, in the vanity of their mind, having the understanding darkened, being alienated from the life of God through the ignorance that is in them, because of the blindness of their heart: who being past feeling-

That is a terrible expression: "past feeling"-

Ephesians 4:19-25. Have given themselves over unto lasciviousness, to work all uncleanness with greediness. But ye have not so learned Christ; if so be that ye have heard him, and have been taught by him, as the truth is in Jesus: that ye put off concerning the former conversation the old man, which is corrupt according to the deceitful lusts; and be renewed in the spirit of your mind; and that ye put on the new man, which after God is created in righteousness and true holiness. Wherefore putting away lying,

As a rotten, worn-out garment that you could not bear to wear,-

Ephesians 4:26. Speak every man truth with his neighbor: for we are members one of another.

Then, why should we lie one to another? Should one hand try to deceive the other hand? Should the eye mislead the foot? Surely, the union of one member with all the other members should ensure its truthfulness.

Ephesians 4:26. Be ye angry, and sin not:

If you must be angry, (and you must, sometimes,) take care that you do not sin when you are angry. It is rather a difficult thing to be angry, and not to sin; yet, if a man were to see sin, and not to be angry with it, he would sin through not being angry. If we are only angry, in a right spirit, with a wrong thing, we shall manage to obey the injunction of the apostle: "Be ye angry, and sin not:"

Ephesians 4:26. Let not the sun go down upon your wrath:

Never let it outlive the day, but forgive ere the sun goes down.

Ephesians 4:27. Neither give place to the devil.

A man who harbours malice in his heart, invites the devil to come in, and keeps a place ready for him.

Ephesians 4:28. Let him that stole steal no more: but rather let him labour,-
For laziness is generally the cause of theft. If a man would work for what he wanted, he would not be tempted to steal it. Paul carries his argument very far, "let him labour,"-

Ephesians 4:28. Working with his hands the thing which is good, that he may have to give to him that needeth.
What a rise there is here,-from a thief up to a giver to him that needeth! This is what the grace of God does. Here is a man, who used to take his neighbor's goods if he could; but, when grace transforms him, he actually gives a share of his own goods to his poor neighbor; that is a marvelous change.

Ephesians 4:29. Let no corrupt communication proceed out of your mouth,-
I have heard unthinking people say, "Well, if it is in your heart, you may as well speak it; it is better out than in." I do not agree with them! If you had a barrel of whiskey in your house, that would certainly be a bad thing to be in your possession; but it would not do any hurt so long as you kept it unopened, so that nobody could get at it, for the mischief arises when people begin to drink it. Undoubtedly, it is an evil thing for you to have anything that is corrupt in your heart, but it will not be mischievous to other people until it begins to come out; so, "let no corrupt communication proceed out of your mouth,"-

Ephesians 4:29. But-
Since some communication is sure to come out of your mouth, let it be a good one,-

Ephesians 4:29-31. That which is good to the use of edifying, that it may minister grace unto the hearers. And grieve not the holy Spirit of God, whereby ye are sealed unto the day of redemption. Let all bitterness, and wrath, and anger, and clamor, and evil speaking, be put away from you, with all malice:
Especially take heed of that "evil speaking" against which the apostle warns you, for there are many people who cannot live without speaking; they must talk a great deal, and they often say that which is false; they invent evil, they twist an honest action, and impute wrong motives to the doer of it. A few such persons in a community can cause much of heartache and distress; they little know what servants of Satan they may become. God help us to put away all evil speaking, and all malice!

Ephesians 4:32. And be ye kind one to another, tenderhearted, forgiving one another, even is God for Christ's sake hath forgiven you.
That is, very freely, very often, very abundantly, very thoroughly, very heartily: "even as God for Christ's sake hath forgiven you," so also do ye.

EPHESIANS CHAPTER 5

Verses 1-33

Ephesians 5:1. Be ye therefore followers of God,
Or, imitators of God,-

Ephesians 5:1. As dear children;
Children are naturally imitators. They are usually inclined to imitate their father; this is, therefore, a most comely and appropriate precept: "Be ye therefore imitators of God, as dear children."

Ephesians 5:2. And walk in love, as Christ also hath loved us, and hath given himself for us, an offering and a sacrifice to God for a sweet smelling savor.
What a path to walk in! "Walk in love." What a well-paved way it is! "As Christ also hath loved us." What a blessed Person for us to follow in that divinely royal road! It would have been hard for us to tread this way of love, if it had not been that his blessed feet marked out the track for us. We are to love as Christ also hath loved us and the question which will often solve difficulties is this, "What would Jesus Christ do in my case? What he would have done, that we may do: "Walk in love, as Christ also hath loved us." And if we want to know how far that love may be carried, we need not be afraid of going too far in self-denial; we may even make a sacrifice of ourselves for love of God and men, for here is our model: "As Christ also hath loved us, and hath given himself for us, an offering and a sacrifice to God for a sweet-smelling savor."

Ephesians 5:3. But fornication, and all uncleanness, or covetousness, let it not be once named among you, as becometh saints;
So far from ever falling under the power of these evils, do not even name them; count them sins unmentionable to holy cars. In what a position do we find "covetousness" placed, side by side with "fornication end all uncleanness"! In the Epistle to the Colossians, covetousness is called "idolatry", as if the Holy Spirit thought so ill of this sin that line could never put it in worse company than it deserved to be in. Yet I fear it is a very common sin even amongst some who call themselves saints. God deliver us altogether from its sway, and help us to hate the very name of it!

Ephesians 5:4. Neither filthiness, nor foolish talking, nor jesting, which are not convenient but rather giving of thanks.
All sorts of evil, frivolous, fruitless talk should be condemned by the Christian. He should feel that he lives at a nobler rate, he lives to purpose; he lives to bear fruit; and that which has no fruit about it, and out of which no good can come, is not for him. "But rather giving of thanks." Oh, for more of this giving of thanks! It should perfume the labours of the day, it should sweeten the rest of the night, this giving of thanks. We are always receiving blessings; let us never cease to give God thanks for them. If we never leave off thanking until we are beyond the need of blessing, we shall go on praising the Lord as long as we live here, and continue to do so throughout eternity.

Ephesians 5:5. For this ye know, that no whoremonger, nor unclean person, nor covetous man, who is an idolater, hath, any inheritance in the kingdom of Christ and of God.

What a sweeping sentence! This is indeed a sword with two edges. Many will flinch before it; and yet, though they flinch, they will not escape, for Paul speaks neither more nor less than the truth when he declares that "no whoremonger, nor unclean person, nor covetous man, who is an idolater, hath any inheritance in the kingdom of Christ and of God."

Ephesians 5:6. Let no man deceive you with vain words for because of these things cometh the wrath of God upon the children of disobedience.

These are the very things God hates. If, therefore, they are in you, God cannot look upon you with the love that he feels towards his children. "These things" he cannot endure, and "because of these things cometh the wrath of God upon the children of disobedience."

Ephesians 5:8. Be not ye therefore partakers with them. For ye were sometimes darkness,

Then, "these things" suited you.

Ephesians 5:8. But now are ye light in the Lord: walk as children of light;

Get clean away from these dark things; travel no more in the thick gloom of these abominations. God help you to walk in the light as he is in the light!

Ephesians 5:9-10. (For the fruit of the Spirit is in all goodness and righteousness and truth;) proving what is acceptable unto the Lord.

We ought to pray that our whole life may be "acceptable unto the Lord." We are ourselves "accepted in the Beloved; " and, that being the case, it should be our great desire that every thought and word and deed, ay, every breathing of our life, should be "acceptable unto the Lord."

Ephesians 5:11-12. And have no fellowship with the unfruitful works of darkness, but rather reprove them. For it is a shame even to speak of those things which are done of them in secret.

It was so with the old heathen world in which Paul lived; he could not write or speak of those abominable vices, which defiled the age. But is London any better than Ephesus? Surely, old Corinth, which became a sink of sin, was not a worse Sodom than this great modern Babylon. There is great cause to say of the wicked even to this day, "It is a shame even to speak of those things which are done of them in secret."

Ephesians 5:13. But all things that are reproved are made manifest by the light;

Then drag them to the light! There will be a great howling when these dogs of darkness have the light let in upon them, but it has to be done.

Ephesians 5:13-15. For whatsoever doth make manifest is light. Wherefore he saith, Awake thou that sleepest, and arise from the dead, and Christ shall give thee light.
See then that ye walk circumspectly, Not carelessly, not thinking that it is of no importance how you live; but looking all round you, "walk circumspectly," watching lest even in seeking one good thing you spoil another. Never present to God one duty stained with the blood of another duty. "See then that ye walk circumspectly,"-

Ephesians 5:15-16. Not as fools, but as wise, redeeming the time,
Buying up the hours; they are of such value that you cannot pay too high a price for them.

Ephesians 5:16-18. Because the days are evil. Wherefore be ye not unwise, but understanding what the will of the Lord is. And be not drunk with wine, wherein is excess; but be filled with the Spirit;
If you want excitement, seek this highest, holiest, happiest form of exhilaration, the divine exhilaration which the Holy Spirit alone can give you: "Be filled with the Spirit."

Ephesians 5:19. Speaking to yourselves in psalms and hymns and spiritual songs, singing and making melody in your heart to the Lord;
We should have thought that Paul would have said, "singing and making melody with your voice to the Lord;" but the apostle, guided by the Holy Ghost, overlooks the sound, which is the mere body of the praise, and looks to the heart, which is the living soul of the praise: "Making melody in your heart to the Lord," for the Lord careth not merely for sounds, though they be the sweetest that ever came from the lip of man or angel; he looks at the heart. God is a Spirit, and he looks spiritually at our spiritual praises; therefore, let us make melody in our heart to the Lord.

Ephesians 5:20-21. Giving thanks always for all things unto God and the Father in the name of our Lord Jesus Christ; submitting yourselves one to another in the fear of God.
That principle of maintaining your rights, standing up for your dignity, and so on, is not according to the mind of the Spirit. It is his will that you should rather yield your rights, and, for the sake of peace, and the profit of your brethren, give up what you might naturally claim as properly belonging to you: "Submitting yourselves one to another in the fear of God."

Ephesians 5:22-30. Wives, submit yourselves unto your own husbands, as unto the Lord. For the husband is the head of the wife, even as Christ's is the head of the church and he is the Saviour of the body. Therefore as the church is subject unto Christ, so let the wives be to their own husbands, in every thing. Husbands, love your wives, even as Christ also loved the church, and gave himself for it; that he might sanctify and cleanse it with the washing of

27

water by the word, that he might present it to himself a glorious church, not having spot, or wrinkle, or any such thing; but that it should be holy and without blemish. So ought men to love their wives as their own bodies. He that loveth his wife loveth himself. For no man ever yet hated his own flesh; but nourisheth and cherisheth it, even as the Lord the church; for we are members of his body, of his flesh, and of his bones,
What a wonderful expression! To think that we, poor creatures that we are, should be thus joined to Christ by a marriage union, nay, by a vital union,-is indeed amazing. Oh, the depths of the love of Christ, that such an expression as this should be possible!

Ephesians 5:31-32. For this cause shalt a man leave his father and mother, and shall be joined unto his wife, and they two shall be one flesh. This is a great mystery: but I speak concerning Christ and the church.
There is the mystery, that he should leave his Father, and quit the home above, and become one flesh with his elect, going with them, and for their sakes, through poverty, and pain, and shame, and death. This is a marvel and a mystery indeed.

Ephesians 5:33. Nevertheless, let every one of you in particular so love his wife even as himself, and the wife see that she reverence her husband.
Thus the Spirit of God follows us to our homes, and teaches us how to live to the glory of God. May he help us so to do, for Christ's sake! Amen.

EPHESIANS CHAPTER 6

Verses 1-15

Ephesians 6:1. Children, obey your parents in the Lord: for this is right.
Fitting by nature, and pleasing in the sight of God.

Ephesians 6:2-4. Honour thy father and mother; which is the first
commandment with promise: That it may be, well with thee, and thou mayest
live long on the earth. And ye fathers, provoke not your children to wrath: but
bring them up in the nurture and admonition of tire Lord.
For the duties are like birds with two wings, or like a pair of scales, balance for
each side. There is the child's duty, but there is the parent's duty too.

Ephesians 6:5-9. Servants, be obedient to them that are your masters
according to the flesh, with fear and trembling, in singleness of your heart, as
unto Christ;
Not with eyeservice, as menpleasers; but as the servants of Christ, doing the
will of God from the heart; With good will doing service, as to the Lord, and not
to men: Knowing that whatsoever good thing any man doeth, the saint shall he
receive of the Lord, whether he be bond or free. And, ye masters, do the same
things unto them, Mind that. We may hear a good deal about the dairies of
servants. Let us hear something about are duties of masters and mistresses.
"Ye masters, do the same things unto them."

Ephesians 6:9. Forbearing threatening: knowing that your Master also is in
heaven; neither is there respect of persons with him.
Very beautifully balanced is the whole system of gospel morals. There is no
undue advantage given by the fact of our being rendered equal in Christ, so
that the servant is to be less obedient to the master, or the child to the parent;
neither is there any undue power given to those who are in authority; but the
grace of God teaches all to do unto all as we would that they should do unto
us.

Ephesians 6:10. Finally, my brethren, be strong in the Lord,
You cannot do right if you are not strong. Unless you have the backbone of
principle — unless you have spiritual muscle and sinew by the indwelling of
the Holy Ghost in you, you cannot continue to do that which is right. "Finally,
my brethren, be strong in the Lord."

Ephesians 6:10-11. And in the power of his might. Put on the whole armor of
God,
First, be strong, and then put on armor. It is no use putting armor on a weak
man, or else it will be what James said it was — a capital invention, He said,
because he who wore it would come to no harm, and certainly do no harm, for
he could not stir in it. Now you must be strong first, but then not trust in your
strength, but put on the armor which is here described. And yet it would be
useless to have the armor unless you are first strong. "Put on the whole armor
of God."

Ephesians 6:11; Ephesians 6:13. That ye may be able to stand against the wiles of the devil. For we wrestle not against flesh and blood, but against principalities, against powers, against the rulers of the darkness of this world, against spiritual wickedness in high places. Wherefore take unto you the whole armor of God, that ye may be able to withstand in the evil day, and having done all, to stand.

To keep your ground, not to give way in any respect, and blessed is that man whose name is Stand-fast, and whose practice is to hold fast —"having done all to stand."

Ephesians 6:14. Stand therefore, having your loins girt about with truth,
Nothing will so tighten up your garments and keep them right as a girdle of sincerity and truthfulness. If we are not true, whatever else we are, we are but loosely arrayed. We shall come to mischief. "Having your loins girt about with truth."

Ephesians 6:14. And having on the breastplate of righteousness;
A grand protection when God has given you to be holy, and when the principle which covers your heart and shields your members is righteousness.

Ephesians 6:15. And your feet shod with the preparation of the gospel of peace;
Peace in year own heart, peace with God, peace with man. Peacefulness and peace. No shoes like these. A man that has a merry heart makes many a mile fly beneath him, but a heavy heart is a slow traveler. "Your feet shod with the preparation of the gospel of peace."

This exposition consisted of readings from Ephesians 4. and Ephesians 6:1-15.

Verses 10-24

Ephesians 6:10. Finally, my brethren, be strong in the Lord, and in the power of his might.
Everything depends upon that. Whether you are called upon to work, or to wait, or to watch, or to suffer, you have need to be strong. If you are not yourself strong, the very armor that you wear will be a burden to you. It is of the utmost importance that Christians should be as strong in grace as they can possibly be. And the power that is to be in them is to be the power of God: "the power of his might." What a wonderful power that is! The power of flesh is weakness, and the power of man is fading but the power of God is almighty and unchangeable; and if we can be girt about with this power there is scarcely any limit to what we may successfully attempt. "Finally," — as if this were a matter of the highest importance, to be considered first and last. — "Finally, my brethren, be strong in the Lord and in the power of his might." You know how strong Paul himself was; he was a veritable giant for Christ, and he here calls upon his brethren to be as he was, he did not want to be brother to

dwarfs, so he appealed to his brethren to "be strong in the Lord, and in the power of his might."

Ephesians 6:11. Put on the whole armor of God, —
The armor of God will not serve you unless you yourself are strong. It needs a strong man to carry girdle, and breastplate, and shoes, and shield, and helmet, and sword. Let me impress upon you the fact that we must first of all get strong within, and after that "put on the whole armor of God," that armor which God has provided for the good soldiers of Jesus Christ, that armor which distinguishes men as belonging to the army of God. Do not merely put on a part of it, but put on the whole of it. Do not simply look at the armor, and clean it up so as to keep it bright, but put it on, wear it, it is meant for you to use in the great battle for the right against the wrong: "Put on the whole armor of God," —

Ephesians 6:11. That ye may be able to stand against the wiles of the devil.
He will attack you sometimes by force and sometimes by fraud. By might or by sleight he will seek to overcome you, and no unarmed man can stand against him. Never go out without all your armor on, for you can never tell where you may meet the devil. He is not omnipresent, but nobody can tell where he is not, for he and his troops of devils appear to be found everywhere on this earth.

Ephesians 6:12. For we wrestle not against flesh and blood, —
Our great fight is not against our fellow-men. As Christians, we go not forth armed with sword and shield to fight against "flesh and blood," —

Ephesians 6:12. But against principalities, against powers, against the rulers of the darkness of this world, against spiritual wickedness in high places.
Our battle is against evil wherever it is to be found, against evil in every shape and form. Evil is as much in the world today as it was in Paul's time, and we must fight against it everywhere. We are not to shut our eyes to it, or try to patch up a compromise with it. Christians are bound to fight against evil principalities, evil powers, the evil rulers of the darkness of this world, and wicked spirits in high places.

Ephesians 6:13. Therefore take unto you the whole armor of God,
What stress the apostle lays upon this point! He repeats the command he had just given, and again emphasizes the fact that it is "the whole armor of God" that is to be worn. There are some professing Christians who only in part obey the injunction here given, but it is no use to wear a part of the Christian armor, and to leave the rest of the soul unarmed. A little leak will sink a ship, and the absence of one piece of the armor of God may cost a man his soul: "Wherefore take unto you the whole armor of God," —

Ephesians 6:13. That ye may be able to withstand in the evil day, and having done all, to stand.
That is what we have to do, to keep our place and our standing as Christians right to the end. To be apparently pure and holy for a time is no use at all. Transient professors will find everlasting ruin; "but he that shall endure unto the end, the same shall be saved." We are in God's army for life; we can never quit this warfare till God shall call us home.

Ephesians 6:14. Stand therefore, having your loins girt about with truth, —
Let this girdle of the everlasting truth of God brace you up. Let it tighten all the rest of your armor.

Ephesians 6:14. And having on the breastplate of righteousness;
Let your heart be guarded by the knowledge that you are right with God, — that you love that which is holy and true. Put on the righteousness of Christ himself as the best possible protection for your heart.

Ephesians 6:15. And your feet shod with the preparation of the gospel of peace;
Rough roads grow smooth when these blessed gospel sandals are on your feet. A little stone in the shoe will make the pilgrim's progress a very wearisome and painful one, so try to keep out all the stones, — everything about which you have any scruple, or that you think may be wrong; and walk in the safe and narrow way set forth in the gospel of peace.

Ephesians 6:16. above all, —
Over all, covering all from head to foot, —

Ephesians 6:16. Taking the shield of faith
For you need this shield to protect both your armor and yourself.

Ephesians 6:16. Therewith ye shall be able to quench all the fiery darts of the wicked.
Not only the fiery darts of the wicked one, but those also of wicked men and wicked women who may throw at you afar darts that are all ablaze, which would burn as well as pierce you if you were not well guarded against them. Nothing can quench these fiery darts but the shield of faith.

Ephesians 6:17. And take the helmet of salvation, —
You used to wear the helmet of pride with its fine nodding plumes, but that has been taken off by you long ago. Now put on "the helmet of Salvation." This will effectually defend your head, and no sword will be able to cleave through it to injure you. Your brain and everything that is connected with your mental powers will be right when you know that you are saved, and when the power of God's salvation is working within you.

Ephesians 6:17. And the sword of the Spirit, which is the word of God. There is no sword like that; it pierces even to the dividing asunder of soul and spirit, and of the joints and marrow, and is a discerner of the thoughts and intents of the heart. Nothing can resist the Word of God if it is only wielded aright. There is one more weapon in the heavenly armoury: —

Ephesians 6:18. Praying always with all prayer and supplication in the Spirit, —

When you cannot use your sword, and even when you can hardly grasp your shield, you can pray. That weapon of "all prayer" is of the handiest kind, because it can be turned in any and every direction. "Praying always with all prayer" — groaning prayers, weeping prayers, prayers that are made up of single words, prayers that have not a word in them, prayers for others, prayers of confession, prayers of thanksgiving, — "praying always with all prayer and supplication in the Spirit," —

Ephesians 6:18. And watching thereunto with all perseverance and supplication for all saints;
But will prayer for other people help us? Yes, very much. You will sometimes find that, when you cannot pray for yourself, it is a good plan to pray for somebody else. Think of some child of God, and pray for him, and then the fire of supplication will soon burn up in your heart. The Lord turned the captivity of Job when he prayed for his friends, and he will do the same for you. I have heard many of our members say that, when they have felt bound in prayer, they have pleaded for their Pastor and afterwards they have been able to pray for themselves. I advise more of you to try that plan; it will do me good, and then if it also does you good, there will be a double advantage in it. Paul was of the same mind as I am, for he added, —

Ephesians 6:19-20. And for me, that utterance may be given unto me, that I may open my mouth boldly, to make known the mystery of the gospel, for which I am an ambassador in bonds:
"An ambassador in bonds!" Such a thing was never heard of in earthly courts We never think of chaining an ambassador, but this is how men treated this great messenger from the court of heaven.

Ephesians 6:20-22. That therein I may speak boldly, as I ought to speak. But that ye also may know my affairs, and how I do, Tychicus, a beloved brother and faithful minister in the Lord, shall make known to you all things: whom I have sent unto you for the same purpose, that ye might know our affairs, and that he might comfort your hearts.
It is well for Christian people to know how it fares with their spiritual guides. Paul wished the Ephesian saints to know in what state of heart he found himself, that they might the more intelligently pray for him.

Ephesians 6:23-24. Peace be to the brethren, and love with faith, from God the Father and the Lord Jesus Christ. Grace be with all them that love our Lord Jesus Christ in sincerity. Amen

I am sure that we can heartily repeat that benediction May the Lord send much of his grace to all his people, in every part of the earth, who love him in sincerity! Amen.

Made in the USA
Monee, IL
04 January 2022

87939668R00020